REHEARSAL

REHEARSAL

POEMS

IRENE WILLIS

International Psychoanalytic Books (IPBooks)
New York
IPBooks.net

Copyright © 2018 by Irene Willis

International Psychoanalytic Books (IPBooks)
Queens, NY 11102

Online at: IPBooks.net

All rights reserved. No part of this book may be used or reproduced in any manner whatsoever including Internet usage, without written permission of the author except in the case of brief quotations embodied in critical articles and reviews.

ISBN: 978-1-949093-01-8

for my husband, Bernard Daves Rossell,
(d. 2016), once more and always

Was it you who invented death, blank page?
—D. Nurkse

Contents

I

Rehearsal	1
A New Book	2
Longing	3
Hygge	4
Following	5
Taking Care	6
Last Call	7
Weather	8
Letting Go	9
Josh	10
Un-filling	11
Leaving Alice	12
Passing It On	13
She Knew	14
What Can You Give Me?	15
That Night	16
Gone	17
Cream of Wheat	18
Sorry for Your Loss	19
Later	20
Clipping the Hedge	21
Phone Call	22
This Much	23
Soft Target	24
Widows	25

II

Hers	28
Her Self	29
Objects	30
One Thing a Day	31
Approaching Eighty	32
Under the Weather	33
Slowly I've Turned into the Matriarch	34
The Mother Tree	35
DNA	36
Platitudes at the Gas Pump	37
Gerontology	38
Where They Live Now	39
As We Wait for Dinner	40
Letter to Donald Hall	41
To All the Lost Poets	42
Maxine: Our Last Exchange	43
The Wrong Demographic	44
Endpoint	45
Getting to Choose	46
Notes	47
About the Author	48
Acknowledgments	49

I

Rehearsal

My husband is reading
How We Die (Nuland)
Nothing to Be Frightened of (Barnes)
and *Mortality* (Hitchens)
and the dog is watching him
the dog with gray muzzle and eyebrows
is watching him.
My husband reads cheerfully
and I, who bought the books
he chose from my shelf,
am watching him and the dog.

A New Book

When he finishes
the books on death,
I give my husband
a book about life:
Travels with Epicurus
by Daniel Klein,
who traveled
to a Greek island
where very old men
sit in the sun, play cards
and tell each other
stories—which,
as Muriel Rukeyser said
(and now some scientists
agree) are what the universe
is really made of.
The listeners
already know the stories
but it doesn't matter
or perhaps it matters
because they do.
They talk and listen,
face to face,
drink glass after glass
of ouzo and sun.

Longing

When old, old women up and get the blues
they miss the weathered hands that stroke and slip
fine-fingered down the alabaster hip…
            –Rebecca Meredith

How can we long
for what we already have?

Easy, said the old woman
who sang the lonely blues

while her old man slept
in his chair, the one he loved,

the him she loved, but still
longed for him as he was—

tall and strong, able to do
all that became a man

and as he got older
and older and older

asleep in his chair—
he knew her longing, too.

Hygge

Getting hygge with it: tips on how to relax,
cuddle up, sip cocoa, bake pastries, knit sweaters
and above all—drink coffee.
        –Judith Newman in The NY Times Book Review

Well, what do you know, the Danes have a word
for it—that warm feeling I always have at dusk
when, curtains drawn, blinds down, we settle in
and snuggle with our cocoa or our tea,
dog on a lap or curled up at our feet.

Those caffeinated connoisseurs of happiness
pronounce it *hoo-ga*—sound of Daddy's horn
on the roadster with the rumble seat for me.
Hoo-ga when it waited at the curb. Then
hoo-ga when they came to take it away.

Hoo-ga sounding like a hug. Or, as he
would say when he came to tuck me in,
"snug as a bug in a rug"—quilt to my chin.
Hoo-ga, hoo-ga as I closed my eyes—
hoo-ga, hooga—till I woke again.

Following

I think I'm following you
I said to my beloved
into old age.

I've been waiting for you,
he said, holding out
his hand.

Taking Care

I didn't know it would be like this
but what I know now is

every day he comes downstairs
alive, I count myself lucky.

Is this what "taking care of" means?
If so, it's okay.

I take care.
He lets me.

Last Call

It's ten p.m.
and my dog is telling me what to do.

You can't go to bed, she says,
until Davey has his pills,

and I can't
until you have your cocoa,
so Sit! Stay!
till I tell you it's okay.

That's better. Good girl.

I know everything that's done
in this house
and the mouse
that lives under the tv

is my friend.

Weather

The weather's unkind today
my husband says
looking skyward for solace
as he often does.

We pace each other now
to see who can last longer.
I work to keep him alive;
he thinks I'm okay

as he always has, while I
try to *stay* okay to keep him
thinking that—and *will*
if the weather holds.

Letting Go

Does there come a time
when you're beyond embarrassment?

Is all that part of letting go
and the rehearsal for letting go?

I try to preserve his dignity
but he's beyond that.

Courage means more

Josh

Old, we rely on people
to "help us out," as they say—
but really to do *whatever,*
which is most, that we can't
do ourselves. I get up early
to let in the furnace man
and, to my surprise, it's Josh,
the one who cuts our grass
and blows our leaves away.
Winters, he's our shoveler
now that Harry's gone.
And when we push the button
on our "Link to Life,"
I daresay the one who
shows up at the door
won't be a stranger, either—
might be Josh.

Un-filling

Is this what the psyche does—
prepare for death the way
a young girl fills—or used to
fill a hope chest?

Because right now—un-filling
is what I do—clearing out
detritus from my life
so I can see it through.

Leaving Alice

A cry of anguish as I leave the house…
Alice, my dog of thirteen years
ninety-one in human terms, and nearly
blind. Her world, the vet says, seen
through dark glasses. I used to celebrate
her independence, but now she clings
as if each separation means forever.
I always say a careful goodbye before
going down our path to get the mail,
tell her we'll meet outside as I go
out the front and she through her own
back door, but still she cries until
I'm in her view and she in mine. I find
it tears me too.

Passing It On

–for Olivia

A friend asked, "How can such
a happy dog look so sad?"

"I think someone broke her heart
four centuries ago," 1 said, "and she's

carried that memory down
through the years, passing it on

to every Springer Spaniel since,
all look-alikes throughout the world—

lively, loving dogs with sad eyes,
mourning what it was that made them so."

She Knew

I think she knows, I said to the vet.

She doesn't know anything, he said.
She's a dog. Don't anthropomorphize.

But she did. I know she did.
Something bad is happening to her,
she'd heard him say, and she knew
bad and *her.*

When he left.the room, she came
and clawed my lap, pleading,
Let's go home.

We thought about an obit piece,
even tried to write one, but decided
the world would think us smart-ass
and instead descended

into our own *anthropomorphia*—
wrapping our arms around each other
where her emptiness now was—
dreaming her, seeing her shade.

What Can You Give Me?

Golden minutes.

Count them out with a spoon.

Pray that the glitter lasts

till noon.

That Night

He was picking up the phone
to make a couple of appointments:

the first with a new dermatologist
because he said the other was "too old;"

the second, with the restaurant for our
anniversary, at the place we both liked best

and where I always took him for his birthday,
which that year would be his ninety-sixth.

Nobody told him he would die soon.
Nobody told me.

And nobody told either one of us
that it would begin that night

while I was asleep in our bedroom
and he was falling from his chair.

Gone

Bathrobe hanging on its hook.
Laptop open in the breakfast nook.
How can he be gone?
He's gone.

Books piled up beside his chair.
Mail coming in as if he's there.
How can he be gone?
He's gone.

Dog lying down at empty feet.
Both of us afraid to take his seat.
How can he be gone?
He's gone.

Bed still rumpled where he slept.
Unfinished puzzle that I've kept.
How can he be gone?
He's gone.

Will he still get in if he comes back?
It wasn't even a real heart attack.
How can he be—is he really gone?
I can't believe, even though I try,

That someone so alive and loved
could die.

Cream of Wheat

Surely one of the blessings of life
is hot water—gushing from the tap,
filling the tub as we step in—
second only to a roof over one's head
or a hot meal, a warm bed.

He loved everything the nurses did—
the hot shave that made his face pink
and the cream of wheat that took him back
to infancy when spoon-fed by his mother.
He thanked them all each time, as he did me.

He didn't know he was dying then
but as he would have said, in the wisdom
of his years, "We're all dying every day.
We're born to die; that's how it is."

I wish I had known he loved cream of wheat.

Sorry for Your Loss

A routine phrase like have-a-nice-day
even on a dreary afternoon

or early evening when I leave the store.
But flowers she brought me didn't die;

her cookies and soup gave sustenance
and nourished what of me was still alive.

I'm here, it said, a voice that kept on singing
like the furnace in the empty house, still warm.

Later

A friend sent flowers
called "Canterbury Bells"

that arrived together
with their lips closed

but opened later
into greater loveliness—

purple, white—
and joy each morning

as the sun rose.

Clipping the Hedge

Pack of Pall Malls and a lighter on my doorstep.
Our yard man, who's already lost one lung,
stashes his smokes within reach before he starts,

and saddens me, sensing he will go like this.
I want to warn him not to try this time
as he takes it upon himself to clip our hedge,

but work is what he knows and what he does,
however little he may earn from us—
and I must admit the *clip-clip* offers comfort,

yet wonder, as I cough, catching my breath,
whether he or I will be the one that's next.
Aging, we need helpers more, it seems.

Today it's Harry. Tomorrow it may be Josh,
who shows up everywhere and mans the plow.
Or are all the young ones now named Josh

and will I see this winter into spring?

Phone Call

I thought, when she spelled h-o-s
that she was on a new medicine,

but she, in a garbled way,
was spelling *hospice*.

Can't recall what I said next
to make my dear friend laugh

but she did. Friend who always
told me, "Spring will come."

This Much

Old, she went to bed alone
and dreamed of dead lovers,

the touch of each distinct
as leaves in a garden of flowers,

as fingers on keys striking notes.
About it I can say this much:

Her ears had memories, too—
but what she dreamed was touch.

Soft Target

My baby my baby I heard
my father cry after the sharp
sting in my right thigh and my
own sharp cry at seven when
for once I didn't mind being
called a baby as he lifted me
in his arms, laid me down
gently on the ground, dabbed
the blood and dressed the wound.
Knew how to dress the wound.
I had a wound and I was proud.
A bullet wound, like the soldier
I had always wanted to be
and I didn't think to blame him
although my mother did
for having his senior campers
build a bonfire after the carnival
and the target shoot that was
part of it. A live bullet, I learned
later, got swept up with debris
and he was—a word I know now—
inconsolate. My brave father
crying as he bandaged and
picked me up again.

Widows

My widowed friends
tell me they still talk
to their dead husbands

which used to shock me.

Not any more.

My dog and I
expect to go to the door
any day now
and find him there.

II

Hers

At some point after he died
she started to own her own life.

What did it mean, to own a life?
She couldn't explain it, but she knew

who she was, was not who she had been;
where she was, was not the same.

If she woke in that house, the house was hers;
if she slept there now, it was where she was.

If the bed was hard, she could up and leave.
If the bed was soft, it was hers to change.

If she saw him now, her mind was still.
But her mind was hers, and hers alone.

Her Self

The self exists within the objects it has cherished,
to be resurrected there'
            –Christopher Bollas

And so, *her* mother's egg cup of plain white
china on a kitchen shelf beside my mother's
cream pitcher with hand-painted ivy and the
hidden crack that always spilled its contents
as she did secrets. In my dresser drawer
the tiny knitted booties with stitched-on pearls
that her best friend Nellie made for her when
she was old, and at my back door now, her cane.
Warming my knees, the jewel-toned afghan
she herself crocheted with skill she didn't
seem to have when I was growing up.
Can it be that she is here, hidden within egg cup,
pitcher, booties, afghan? Mother—*here*?
I think I've always known. Lately, I see her
everywhere. Driving by, hair the same permed
reddish-brown. Walking with the cane, holding
onto a daughter's arm. Seated in a restaurant,
(cheekbones, nose, the angle of her chin).
Why now, when she's been gone so long?
What objects will hold *me*, my own end near?

Objects

Sorting out objects that define your life
you find out who you are—

or you don't.

What they *are* is irremediable;
What they're *not* is real.

Was I this person in the album?
Am I the one who signed my name?

Is she here now or someone other,
the resident of a country called Old Age,

learning a new language of the body,
defining a different sense of self?

Was I the *she*

that packed these things into boxes
to be sorted out after the downsize—

and later, final downsize, into ash?

One Thing a Day

I'm beginning to know how my mother felt
in the years when she could do "one thing a day."
Some days it was to go to the coffee shop,
where she had one cup with four packets of Equal,
then slipped more in her purse to use at home.
Other days her helper drove her to the bank
so she could see the teller to ask for her balance.
Others for the dentist, doctor, beauty shop,
but never more than that "one thing."
"One thing" the Rx for longevity.
"One thing "the Rx for good health.
"One thing to ward off dementia, poverty.
"One thing to answer when I'd say,
"So tell me, Mommy—what did you do today?"

Approaching Eighty

Was it true, as my mother said,
that if she told anyone her real age
no one would want to be her friend?

As if age were a contagious disease
in which skin, bones, organs
lose their harmonies, and all

that's left is need—desire
so great it terrifies?

Under the Weather

Am I really sick, or just
grieving?

Is grieving ever "just?"

Is justice done when I
look up and see the sky
as it fills up with sun?

Is now the time to stop
and move into the day?

And if I can't, what then?

Slowly I've Turned into the Matriarch

Gifts in tow, they tumble from the van,
nieces and nephews ready to take a look
now that I'm ancestral and they've grown.

Slowly, I've turned into the matriarch.
I feel it creeping up my legs like stone,
knees now angled to the floor

to make a lap in case a little one
should toddle in with something like a book
that needs to be read aloud to be understood

with pictures for the looking and the turning,
like those in the big album I've uncovered—
the ones with pages black from the beginning

and blurry snapshots sliding from their slots.

The Mother Tree

Too old to chain, the tree man said.
It should come down. Dead inside.
But I resisted, though another limb
had crashed, just missing the roof.
How old is it? I asked. *About eighty-five,*
he said, all of twenty-five himself. *But
that's young, isn't it? For a tree?* I said,
patting the thick trunk, looking up
through leaved branches, thinking
I was always younger than the tree I thought
would survive us when we bought the house,
this tree the reason—or one of them.
I looked at it every morning at breakfast,
carried coffee out to sit under it afternoons,
loved the way it shaded where it stood.
Not this kind, the young man said,
and repeated, *It's dead inside.* His final
argument. I gave in. Yesterday six men
arrived in hard white hats, green shirts,
and milled about in serious conference.
*Get rid of the debris, I said, but save
the mother part.* What I have now
is a five-foot-wide stump—orange,
like half of a giant pumpkin, the kind
my mother would never bake into pies.
I lost her long before she died at eighty-five.

DNA

I was so impatient when my mother
walked like this, the way I'm walking now—

the cane a bare necessity, but still,
she began at eighty, deciding to be old,

then gave it up at eighty-five.
Will I outlast, as I'm determined to,

or will the genome have its way with me?
Unruly crew of chromosomes, my DNA.

Platitudes at the Gas Pump

One of the things I never learned to do
is pump my own gas. I know, I know
it's a life skill now, but wasn't "back
in the day," as they say, which was mine.

Maybe because I remember a time
and place where it wasn't allowed
or maybe I thought something about it
was "unladylike." (Did I really just say that?)

That was before Title IX—before almost
everything, I guess. Yes, I admit it; I'm *old*—
not one of the youngest old any more, but one
who is counting the years she has left

with still so much to do and afraid
she can't get it done in time, which is
really the story of my life. *My life*—
little of it I have left, I say,

hoping you'll hear me better
than I hear myself. Where was I?
Oh, yes. Platitudes at the gas pump.
Weather talk. Social interaction.

Rx, I gather, for a longer life.

Gerontology

She wanted to talk.
She wanted to talk
about what she remembered
and what she thought now
but her son said, "You've
told me that already," or
"I've heard that story before."
She wanted to talk
about the review of a book
about an old woman with
medicine bottles lining her
windowsill and post-it notes
saying things like *hairdresser's
name* is *William; yardman's
name* is *George,* and how her
husband, busy with his own
aging, spent his days upstairs
at the computer screen
and nights downstairs
at the TV with a bowl of cereal
sometimes napping
in his chair till dawn
after getting up three times
in the night—once because
of a dream he didn't tell her
about but she knew and
remembered, because
she had dreamed it herself
that night and the night before.

Where They Live Now

They are bragging, bragging—
about what they were and did,
where they traveled, lived.

Tiresome, tiresome, until I see
or think I do—why
they *must:* because here and now

they don't know who they are—
like the woman with mad face,
who rolled her wheelchair up

by my good ear, "Kids! They rob
you blind, then dump you
in a place like this."

I heard, and for the first time knew
how much she needed
to be loved and listened to.

As We Wait for Dinner

among wheelchairs, canes and walkers
I listen for stories at the retirement home—

not wanting to hear once more how *she* baby-sat
the great man or he was regional sales director—

but ready for the tale of eighty years ago
when, paid by his grandmother to take that

boy of six by train from California to New York,
the sitter got off at Las Vegas with some guy she'd

picked up and all of the grandmother's money,
leaving the kid staring out from his window seat

and wondering, not *if* she'd come back but *when*.
Now he stops and coughs, then grins, and tells us

how "the blacks," as he still calls them, looked
after him the whole long rest of the way home.

Letter to Donald Hall

I've heard you read more than once.
I have most of your books, signed.
The last time I saw you I took them
and stood on line to say," I'll bet you
haven't seen this one in a long time;
would you sign it?" And you said,
"I'll sign all of them,"—graciously—

And now you've unpacked your boxes
in Grandpa Wesley's house, Jane is gone
and you say, in *Essays after Eighty,*
that all you can write is prose.

I'm sorry you think your poetry's gone
and you can now govern only in prose.
You did a great job with your new *Selected*;
your taste hasn't left you at all.

But what I wish you would do for us now
is push open that door, go outside and
kick the leaves again. Bring back
a bright new poem—the poem of a
ninety-year-old, in bloom.

To All the Lost Poets

In memoriam, Philip Levine, 1925–2015

NEA, NEH, drying up like
old wells and poets dying.

Poets dying and old ones
still writing but resorting

to governing in prose
that may sing but isn't

the poetry they once wrote,
having decided on their own

that the harp is silent
and the Muse long gone.

Now that I'm old, what
can I do but join them,

that crew of disappearing,
and I still unworthy, un-

deserving, underserved?

Maxine: Our Last Exchange

In memoriam, Maxine Kumin, 1925–2013

My pipes froze, I said in an e-mail.
Left a window open by mistake.

Of course, she said. *Everyone knows
when it's below twenty you drain the pipes.*

I thought below zero, I said, *but no matter.
Did your Suzy get the revised poem I sent?*

I gave it to her, she said, *but right now
she's dealing with frozen pipes herself.*

How did we sign off? I'll look it up.
Luckily, I don't delete too much

and anyway, I wouldn't delete Maxine.
I couldn't delete Maxine.

The Wrong Demographic

—*for Dame Judi Dench*

My favorite actress
about my age but O so wonderful—
turned down by four talk shows
because she's the "wrong
demographic."

O misery! O bullshit!
What idiots adorn the airwaves
and the blatherboxes? What idiots
own and watch and listen?

Did we do this, Survivors all?
Did we in our heartless, made-over
innocence?

Endpoint

What made them turn against us at the end—
those women who always had so much to give?

My mother who left everything and then
cancelled it all—even the policy

with the tiny premium I surely could have paid
and the secondary medical with a few good bits.

And Nana, naming me her executor.
or as she said, *execu-trix,* and then

deciding to take it back and leaving me
only a letter that said I wasn't hers

nor was my father—no "kin," she said, at all.
Was *that* the reason, shocking as it was,

or was it something else, like loneliness,
that desperate feeling at the end of life

that no one cares, that we will die alone
and probably un-mourned, that no one cares?

No one at all, so here's what I will do
to make sure that they all, every one

whoever might have known me, knows:
write my obit now—so I can hope

a few might gather as I Exit Right.

Getting to Choose

But who gets to choose this ordered end…
  —Maxine Kumin

Trying to will an ordered end
I'm mucking out the garage
where old manuscripts are stored

with books, journals, magazines,
old photographs of boyfriends,
husbands, friends' kids, mine.

My bed and board can't survive
this hoard, nor can I abide
leaving it to my only child to sort

and deal with, short of tossing
it all or calling the junkman
and stuffing what remains

into garbage bags for shredding—
if shredding isn't too dear—
but junk won't keep me here.

My ordered end will be
as sparse as I can make it—
the devil take it!

Notes

The epigraph, 'Was it you who invented death, blank page?" is the last line of D. Nurkse's poem, "Notes from the Foothills" in his collection *A Night in Brooklyn* (Alfred A. Knopf, 2013).

Pronunciation and definition of *hygge* are from Wiking, Meik (CEO of the Happiness Research Institute, Copenhagen) *The Little Book of Hygge: Danish Secrets to Happy Living* (William Morrow, 2017).

The poem "Getting to Choose" was inspired by a line from Maxine Kumin's "Allow Me," the last poem in her collection *And Short the Season,* published posthumously (W.W. Norton & Co., 2014).

The epigraph that begins 'When old, old women up and get the blues..." by Rebecca Meredith, appears in Salman Akhtar's *Fifteen Poems by Psychoanalysts* (Karmac Books, 2012)

The epigraph before the poem "Objects" is from Bollas, Christopher, *Being a Character: Psychoanalysis & Self Experience* (Hill and Wang, 1994).

The lines about Suzy and the revised poem in "Maxine: Our Last Exchange" refer to my yet-to-be-published "Dialogue in Green, for Will Barnet." Maxine Kumin's helper, Suzy, was a friend of the family of the Massachusetts artist, my favorite. "It's a fine poem," Maxine said, as I recall; "Suzy will love it."

"Letter to Donald Hall" was never actually sent; it was just what I wanted to say to him after reading his *Essays after Eighty.* His breakthrough book was *Kicking the Leaves.*

About the Author

Irene Willis with her husband, Daves Rossell

IRENE WILLIS is the author of four previous collections of poetry: *They Tell Me You Danced* (University Press of Florida, 1995); *At the Fortune Café,* winner of the Violet Reed Haas Prize and National Book Award nominee (Snake Nation Press, 2005); *Those Flames* (Bay Oak, 2009), and *Reminder* (Word Poetry, 2014). She is also the editor of an anthology, *Climate of Opinion: Sigmund Freud in Poetry* (IPBooks, 2017). Three times nominated for Pushcart Prizes, her poems have appeared in many journals and anthologies. She has also co-authored a number of textbooks and children's books. A longtime educator who has "retired" three times, she has taught at a number of secondary schools and colleges, most recently at Westfield State University and American International College in Massachusetts. Awards for her poetry include a Distinguished Artist fellowship from the New Jersey State Council on the Arts; a residency fellowship from the Millay Colony for the Arts, and grants from the Massachusetts Cultural Council and the Berkshire/Taconic Foundation. She is Poetry Editor of the online publication, *International Psychoanalysis,* where she has a monthly column, "Poetry Monday."

Acknowledgments

Grateful acknowledgment is made to the editors of the following publications in which some of these poems appeared:

The Aurorean: "Maxine: Our Last Exchange"

The Bark: "Last Call," "Leaving Alice"

Berkshire Magazine: "Rehearsal" (reprinted from upstreet)

International Psychoanalysis: "Mother's Day"

The Mind's Eye: "The Mother Tree"

upstreet: "Rehearsal"

U.S. 1 Worksheets: "Un-filling," "Widows"

Women's Review of Books: "Her Self," "Getting to Choose"

I am forever grateful for the supportive fellowship of Lisken Van Pelt Dus, Cynthia Gardner, Zara Raab, Hilary Russell and Phil Timpane and our sole UK member, Chris Fogg, who never stops cheering us on.

Special thanks and *hygge* to my morning poetry buddy, David Giannini; to my personal assistant, Olivia VanSant; my computer consultant, Ernie Lowell, and my current canine beloved, Abigail, who understands what it is to put one page on top of another.

Gratitude also to Tamar and Larry Schwartz at IPBooks, for always being there and for doing whatever needs to be done, whenever.

www.ingramcontent.com/pod-product-compliance
Lightning Source LLC
Chambersburg PA
CBHW052207110526
44591CB00012B/2119